CENGAGE Learning

Drama for Students, Volume 18

Project Editor: David Galens

Editorial: Anne Marie Hacht, Michelle Kazensky, Ira Mark Milne, Pam Revitzer, Kathy Sauer, Timothy J. Sisler, Jennifer Smith, Carol Ullmann

Research: Michelle Campbell, Tracie Richardson

Permissions: Debra J. Freitas

Manufacturing: Stacy Melson

Imaging and Multimedia: Leitha Etheridge-Sims, Lezlie Light, Dave G. Oblender, Kelly A. Quin, Luke Rademacher

Product Design: Pamela A. E. Galbreath

For more information, contact

Gale
27500 Drake Rd.
Farmington Hills, MI 48331-3535
Or you can visit our Internet site at
http://www.gale.com

While every effort has been made to ensure the
reliability of the information presented in this
publication, The Gale Group, Inc. does not

guarantee the accuracy of the data contained herein. The Gale Group, Inc. accepts no payment for listing; and inclusion in the publication of any organization, agency, institution, publication, service, or individual does not imply endorsement of the editors or publisher. Errors brought to the attention of the publisher and verified to the satisfaction of the publisher will be corrected in future editions.

ISBN 0-7876-6815-X
ISSN 1094-9232

Printed in the United States of America
10 9 8 7 6 5 4 3 2 1

Tartuffe

Molière

1664

Introduction

Molière's play *Tartuffe* (also sometimes referred to as *Tartuffe, or, The Imposter*) is a masterwork by France's most celebrated comic playwright. *Tartuffe* is set in the realm of seventeenth-century Parisian high society during the reign of King Louis XIV.

In *Tartuffe*, Orgon, a wealthy family man, takes in a stranger by the name of Tartuffe to stay in his home. Tartuffe appears to be an extremely pious and devout man of religion, and Orgon regards him almost as a saint. Orgon offers Tartuffe his best food and drink and places the needs of his guest above those of his wife and children. He plans to force his daughter to marry Tartuffe and to disinherit his son in order to make Tartuffe the sole heir to his fortune. All of Orgon's friends and family regard Tartuffe as a con man who only pretends to be of the highest moral authority but who does not practice what he preaches. Orgon is warned that Tartuffe may be deceiving him in order to gain both financially and socially, but Orgon is blind to these warnings. Orgon finally learns that he has been betrayed by his guest when he overhears Tartuffe trying to seduce his wife. However, when he orders Tartuffe to leave his house, Tartuffe seeks revenge by trying to seize all of Orgon's property and to have Orgon arrested. In the end, through the intervention of the King, Tartuffe is arrested, and harmony is restored to Orgon's household.

The character of Tartuffe represents those members of society who preach religious piety but do not themselves live by the morals they try to force upon others. Because the play focuses on the issue of religious hypocrisy, it was highly controversial at the time it was written and was banned from public performance for five years.

A translation of *Tartuffe* in verse form by Donald F. Frame is published by Signet Classic in *Tartuffe and Other Plays by Molière* (1967).

Molière, born Jean-Baptiste Poquelin, was baptized in Paris, France, on January 15, 1622. His father was a furniture merchant who, in 1631, was appointed chief provider of furnishings for the home of the king. Molière's mother died when he was ten years old, and in 1633 his father remarried. Molière received his education at the Jesuit Collège de Clermont, after which he studied law and, in 1641, was admitted to the bar. After practicing law for six months, Molière decided to pursue a career in the theater instead. In 1643, he joined the newly formed theater company, the L'Illustre-Théâtre, soon taking the stage name of Molière. In 1645, he joined a touring theater company, with which he traveled throughout the south of France for the next thirteen years. The first public performance of a five-act comedy written by Molière was staged in 1655. In 1657, Molière's theater company, having earned considerable renown as a traveling troupe, moved to Paris. Their first performance before King Louis XIV, *Le Docteur amoureux* (*The Amorous Doctor*), a farce written by Molière himself, was given in 1658. It was a great success with the king, who found it amusing and offered them the patronage of his younger brother, known as "Monsieur." Now called the "troupe de Monsieur," Molière's company was provided performance space in the Petit-Bourbon theater. Molière's first great personal success as an actor and a playwright came with the performance of *Les Précieuses ridicules* (*Such Foolish Affected Ladies*) in 1659. When the Petit-Bourbon was demolished in 1660, the company was given space at the Palais-Royal theater. In 1662, Molière, at age forty, married Armande Béjart, then nineteen years old. That year his comedy, *L'École des femmes* (*The School for Wives* or *The School for Women*), was a popular success but created controversy that continued for over a year. In 1663, Molière was granted a royal pension and, in 1664, King Louis XIV was named godfather of his first-born son, Louis, who died less than a year later. The year 1664 also began a five-year-long controversy over the play *Tartuffe*, which was banned from public performance until 1669. In 1665, Molière's play *Dom Juan* (*Don Juan*) was cancelled after just fifteen performances due to its controversial nature and was never performed again in his lifetime, although it was never officially banned. Nonetheless, that same year the troupe earned the patronage of the king and the appellation Troupe du Roi (The King's Troupe), and Molière's pension was raised considerably. In 1666, while he enjoyed professional successes, Molière's health began to decline seriously, due to tuberculosis, which occasionally prevented him from performing. In 1672, his wife died. A year later, during his performance as the hypochondriac in *Le Malade imaginaire* (1673; *The Hypochondriac* or *The Imaginary Invalid*), Molière collapsed on stage and died later that evening. Although he requested a priest for his final confession, none arrived in time, and, not given the right to a proper funeral because he was an actor, Molière was buried at night.

Plot Summary

Act 1

Tartuffe is set in the Paris home of Orgon, a wealthy man who lives with his wife, Elmire; his daughter, Mariane; and his son, Damis. Orgon also has several houseguests, including Madame Pernelle (his mother), Cléante (Elmire's brother), and Valère, who is engaged to Mariane. Orgon has recently befriended a man named Tartuffe, who has presented himself to Orgon as an extremely pious and devout man. Orgon invites Tartuffe to stay in his home as a moral guide and religious teacher. Orgon regards Tartuffe with extreme reverence, devotion, and adoration and treats him with greater love, affection, and favor than he does his wife and children. Orgon has taken Tartuffe as his close confidante, dotes on his guest excessively, and worships the man as if he were a saint.

In the opening scene, Orgon's mother, Madame Pernelle, announces to the other members of the household that she is leaving to stay elsewhere because she is disgusted with the manner in which they all (except Orgon) criticize Tartuffe. Madame Pernelle advises the others to take Tartuffe's advice and reform their lives, but they protest that there is nothing immoral about their behavior.

Orgon, who has just returned from two days spent in the country, asks Dorine (Mariane's lady's-maid) how everyone has been doing in his absence. Dorine tells him that Elmire, his wife, has been sick, suffering fever, headache, loss of appetite, and insomnia. Orgon, however, expresses no interest in his wife's illness and repeatedly asks about Tartuffe. Dorine describes Tartuffe, in contrast to Elmire, as having been in fine health and having eaten, drunk, and slept excessively. Orgon makes no comment about his wife's suffering and expresses concern only for Tartuffe's well-being.

Orgon describes to Cléante how he met Tartuffe in a church and was so impressed by his piety and virtue that he decided to take the man into his home. Cléante attempts to convince Orgon that Tartuffe is not as virtuous as he pretends to be. He warns Orgon that Tartuffe is using the pretense of religious devotion for the purpose of his own social and material gain. Orgon, however, dismisses Cléante's warnings about Tartuffe.

Act 2

Orgon informs his daughter, Mariane, that he wishes her to marry Tartuffe. Mariane is surprised to hear this, because Orgon had already agreed that she could marry Valère, the man she loves. But Mariane is too obedient to openly protest her father's wishes, and she remains passive while Orgon insists that marrying Tartuffe is a good idea. Dorine, meanwhile, repeatedly interrupts Orgon in an attempt to talk him out of forcing Mariane to marry Tartuffe.

After Orgon leaves the room, Dorine tells Mariane that she must tell her father she refuses to marry Tartuffe because she wishes to marry Valère. Mariane replies that she cannot go against her father's wishes, that she is too timid to fight him for the marriage she wants, and that she will simply kill herself if he forces her to marry Tartuffe. Dorine, however, assures Mariane that they can devise a plan to change Orgon's mind and allow her to marry Valère.

Valère tells Mariane he has heard that she will be marrying Tartuffe. Neither Mariane nor Valère wants to admit to the other to feeling hurt by this change of plans, so they both pretend to be perfectly happy that their engagement has been broken off. However, it is clear that they are both still in love with one another and are merely trying to keep their pride. Dorine then steps in, makes Mariane and Valère hold hands, and forces them to admit that they still love each other. Dorine then assures them that they can devise a plan to gain Orgon's consent to their marriage.

Act 3

Damis, Orgon's son, hides in a closet in order to overhear a conversation between Elmire and Tartuffe. During this conversation, Tartuffe propositions Elmire with the offer of an elicit affair behind her husband's back. He assures Elmire that he would keep her infidelity a secret in order to safeguard his own reputation as a pious man. Elmire lets Tartuffe know that she has no interest in conducting an affair with him. However, she tells him that she will not tell her husband about his sexual advances if he promises to convince Orgon to allow Mariane to marry Valère. At that moment, Damis steps out of the closet where he has been hiding and states that he must report Tartuffe's inappropriate behavior to his father. Elmire pleads with Damis not to tell Orgon of Tartuffe's behavior, but Damis insists that Orgon must be informed of the matter.

Damis tells Orgon that Tartuffe tried to conduct an illicit affair with Elmire. Orgon responds to this information by accusing Damis of lying about Tartuffe's behavior. In his anger, Orgon orders Damis to leave the house immediately and declares that he will disinherit him. Orgon announces that he will make Mariane marry Tartuffe that very night and states that he is going to make Tartuffe the sole heir to his estate.

Act 4

Orgon tells Elmire that he does not believe Tartuffe made a pass at her. Elmire tells Orgon to hide underneath a table in order to overhear her conversation with Tartuffe. While Orgon is hiding under the table, Elmire tells Tartuffe that she would like to have an affair with him. Tartuffe responds that she must prove to him that she is sincere through an act of physical passion. Elmire then asks Tartuffe to look out in the hallway and make sure her husband is not listening in on the conversation. While Tartuffe is out of the room, Orgon comes out from under the table and admits to Elmire that Tartuffe has betrayed him. When Tartuffe returns to the room, Orgon orders him to leave the household immediately. Tartuffe responds that he will get revenge against Orgon for turning against him. Orgon explains to Elmire that he has given Tartuffe certain information that will make it possible for Tartuffe to ruin the family out of revenge.

Act 5

Orgon explains to Cléante that he gave a strongbox containing important documents to Tartuffe for safekeeping. This strongbox had been given to Orgon by a friend who fled the country in order to escape legal problems. Orgon now fears that Tartuffe will use these documents as evidence against him by turning them over to the legal authorities. These documents would serve as evidence that Orgon has been concealing a crime committed by the friend who gave him the strongbox.

Monsieur Loyal, a bailiff, comes to the door and shows Orgon a legal document that names Tartuffe as the rightful owner of the house. He tells Orgon that he must move his family out of the house by the following morning. After Monsieur Loyal leaves, Valère tells Orgon that Tartuffe has handed the strongbox full of incriminating documents over to the King and that there is now a warrant out for Orgon's arrest. Valère has brought a carriage in which Orgon may flee immediately in order to escape arrest.

Before Orgon has a chance to flee, Tartuffe arrives with a Gentleman of the King's Guard and states that Orgon is under arrest. However, just at this moment, the Gentleman of the King's Guard states that he is in fact arresting Tartuffe, not Orgon. The Gentleman of the King's Guard explains that Tartuffe is being arrested for countless crimes he committed under another name. The Gentleman tells Orgon that the King has decided to restore Orgon as rightful owner of his home and wealth and to forgive him for withholding the strongbox of documents.

In the final moments of the play, Orgon decides to go thank the King and then to see to the marriage of Valère and Mariane.

Characters

Cléante

Cléante is the brother of Elmire and brother-inlaw of Orgon. Cléante tries to convince Orgon that Tartuffe is not sincere in his religious devotion and is using Orgon for his money and influence. He observes that Tartuffe makes an outward display of religious devotion but does not practice what he preaches. He points out to Orgon that there are many pious people who live moral lives without making a public display of their piety. Orgon, however, is not convinced by Cléante's reasoning and does not heed his advice about Tartuffe. In the final moments of the play, Cléante advises Orgon to go before the King and thank him for arresting Tartuffe and for restoring Orgon's property to him. He states that Orgon should not harbor ill will toward Tartuffe but should hope that Tartuffe will one day mend his ways and become a truly virtuous person. Many critics have commented that Cléante represents the voice of reason in the play, providing guidelines for the sincere practice of Christian morality in contrast to the false piety of Tartuffe.

Damis

Damis is the son of Orgon, stepson of Elmire, and brother of Mariane. Of all the characters, Damis is the most outraged by Tartuffe's behavior, reacting impulsively and threatening violence on several occasions. Damis is very upset when he learns that Orgon wishes Mariane to marry Tartuffe. Damis is engaged to the sister of Valère and fears that if the engagement between Mariane and Valère is broken, Valère's sister will break her engagement to him as well. Damis hides in a closet in order to overhear the conversation between Tartuffe and Elmire, in which Tartuffe attempts to seduce Elmire. Upon hearing this exchange, Damis becomes extremely upset and goes to tell his father of Tartuffe's behavior. Orgon, however, responds to this information by chastising Damis for daring to speak against Tartuffe. Orgon orders Damis out of the house immediately and declares that he will disinherit his son. Once Orgon learns of Tartuffe's deception, he takes Damis back into the household and wishes to restore his son's rightful inheritance to him. Damis, an emotional and impulsive young man, offers to slay Tartuffe out of revenge but is advised to be patient until a more reasonable plan for dealing with Tartuffe is devised.

Dorine

Dorine is the lady's-maid to Mariane. Although she is a servant, Dorine has a very strong personality and is never afraid to speak out against Orgon or anyone else with whom she disagrees. When Orgon tells Mariane that she must marry Tartuffe, Dorine immediately and emphatically protests the arrangement. She argues with Orgon that if he forces Mariane to marry a man whom she does not love, the result will be that she will be unfaithful to her unwanted husband. Dorine later tells Mariane that she absolutely must stand up to her father and insist that she be allowed to marry Valère, the man whom she loves. Dorine helps to mend the hurt feelings between Mariane and Valère after Valère learns of the engagement to Tartuffe and assures the young lovers that she will devise a plan to allow them to marry one another.

Elmire

Elmire is the wife of Orgon, stepmother of Mariane and Damis, and sister of Cléante. As divorce would have been extremely uncommon in the seventeenth century, the reader is left to assume that Orgon had a first wife who was the mother of Mariane and Damis and that this wife died young. Accordingly, the reader may assume that Elmire is Orgon's second wife. Although Elmire is the stepmother of Mariane and Damis, she seems to treat them as if they were her own children, and they seem to regard her as their mother. In the play, Elmire has a conversation with Tartuffe in which Tartuffe attempts to seduce her into having an affair with him. Elmire politely but clearly refuses Tartuffe's advances. She tells him that she will not tell her husband about his behavior toward her if he promises to convince Orgon to allow Mariane to marry Valère instead of him. This arrangement is foiled when Damis reports this conversation to his father. Because Orgon refuses to believe that Tartuffe tried to seduce his wife, he accuses Elmire of making the story up in order to malign Tartuffe and support the interests of Damis and Mariane. In order to prove to Orgon that Tartuffe has betrayed him, Elmire instructs him to hide underneath a table while she speaks to Tartuffe. While Orgon is hiding, Elmire tells Tartuffe that she would like to have an affair with him, and Tartuffe responds that she must prove this to him through an act of physical passion. At this point, Orgon is convinced that Tartuffe has betrayed him and orders Tartuffe to leave immediately.

Media Adaptations

- *Tartuffe* was adapted to the screen in a 1925 silent film of the same title, directed by the German filmmaker F. W. Murnau and starring Emile Jannings as Tartuffe. This film was released on video with English language intertitles by Grapevine

Video in 1995.

- *Tartuffe; or, The Imposter* was adapted to the screen in a 1984 film of the same title, performed by the Royal Shakespeare Company and directed by Bill Alexander. This production stars Anthony Sher as Tartuffe, Nigel Hawthorne as Orgon, and Alison Steadman as Elmire. It was produced by the British Broadcasting Corporation (BBC) and distributed on video by RKO Home Video.

- *Tartuffe* was adapted to the screen in a 1986 film of the same title, directed by Pierre Badel. This production was performed by the Société des Comédiens Français and was released on video with French dialogue with English language subtitles by Films for the Humanities.

Flipote

Flipote is the maid of Madame Pernelle. Flipote appears only in the opening scene of the play and has no dialogue. As Madame Pernelle is leaving Orgon's house, she slaps Flipote and, calling her a "slut," tells her to hurry up.

A Gentleman of the King's Guard

In the final scene of the play, Tartuffe arrives at Orgon's house with a Gentleman of the King's Guard. Tartuffe announces that they have come to arrest Orgon. However, the Gentleman of the King's Guard informs them that he is in fact going to arrest Tartuffe for various crimes committed under a different name. The Gentleman of the King's Guard also tells Orgon that the King has restored to him all of the property he had signed over to Tartuffe.

The King

Although the King does not appear as a visible presence or speaking character in *Tartuffe*, he is an important offstage character to the plot resolution of the play. Just when Orgon thinks he is about to be arrested, the Gentleman of the King's Guard arrests Tartuffe instead. The Gentleman of the King's Guard explains that the King has pardoned Orgon and will restore his property to him because of the fact that Orgon fought loyally on the side of the King during the civil wars (known as the Fronde). Thus, although the King is not a visible presence onstage, he is significant to the play's theme of loyalty versus betrayal. The ending suggests that loyalty to the King, as well as to one's friends and family, will always be rewarded.

Monsieur Loyal

Toward the end of the play, Monsieur Loyal, a

bailiff, arrives at Orgon's house with a legal document that declares Tartuffe to be the rightful owner of the property. Monsieur Loyal informs Orgon that he and his family must vacate the house by the next morning. Monsieur Loyal adds that he has employed several men to spend the night in the house in order to be sure that they leave in the morning. His name, Loyal, is ironic in that he is in fact disloyal to the King when he acts on Tartuffe's behalf.

Mariane

Mariane is the daughter of Orgon, stepdaughter of Elmire, and sister of Damis. Mariane is in love with Valère and, as the play opens, has been granted her father's permission to marry him. However, Orgon tells her that he wants her to marry Tartuffe instead of Valère. Mariane is horrified by the prospect of having to marry Tartuffe but is too obedient to stand up to her father. She tells Dorine that she will simply kill herself if she is forced to marry Tartuffe. Dorine, however, tells Mariane that she must stand up to her father and insist on marrying Valère;, but when Mariane pleads that she is too afraid to resist her father, Dorine assures her that they will find a way for her to marry Valère. In the final lines of the play, Orgon states that they all must see to the marriage of the "loving pair," Mariane and Valère.

Orgon

Orgon is the husband of Elmire, father of Damis and Mariane, and son of Madame Pernelle. The play takes place in Orgon's home, where he lives with his family and several houseguests. As the play opens, Orgon has met Tartuffe at a church and, impressed with his piety, has invited the stranger to stay in his home indefinitely. Orgon is completely taken with Tartuffe and treats him better than he treats his own family. He regards Tartuffe as his religious guide and is blind to the fact that Tartuffe is deceiving him. When his friends and family try to convince Orgon that Tartuffe is faking his piety and deceiving his host, Orgon dismisses their warnings. In Orgon's eyes, Tartuffe is a model of religious devotion whom all others should emulate. He informs his daughter, Mariane, that he wants her to marry Tartuffe, even though he has already promised that she could marry Valère. When Damis reports to Orgon that Tartuffe has tried to seduce Elmire, his wife, Orgon does not believe him. Instead, Orgon accuses Damis of insulting Tartuffe, orders Damis to leave the house immediately, and announces that he will disinherit his son in order to make Tartuffe his sole heir.

Elmire tells Orgon to hide underneath a table while she talks to Tartuffe so that he will hear for himself what kind of man Tartuffe really is. After Orgon hears Tartuffe trying to seduce Elmire, he is convinced that he has been betrayed. Orgon orders Tartuffe to leave his home immediately, but Tartuffe warns him that he has ample means for getting revenge. Orgon has given Tartuffe a strongbox of papers incriminating himself and has also signed all of his property over to Tartuffe. Thus, Tartuffe arranges to have Orgon arrested and the family turned out of their home. At the end of the play, however, Orgon is informed that he has been pardoned by the King and his property restored to him, while Tartuffe is arrested for a long list of previously committed crimes. In the closing lines of the play, Orgon announces that he will go to the King to thank him and then see to the marriage of Valère and Mariane.

Madame Pernelle

Madame Pernelle is the mother of Orgon, mother-in-law of Elmire, and grandmother of Mariane and Damis. In the opening scene of the play, Madame Pernelle announces that she is leaving Orgon's home because she disapproves of the way the other members of the household (except Orgon) shun Tartuffe. Madame Pernelle criticizes the others for engaging in parties, dances, and other social events, which she considers to be immoral behavior. She tells them all that they should listen to Tartuffe's moral pronouncements against them and try to take his advice. The others protest that there is nothing wrong with socializing with their friends and that Tartuffe is a despicable man who does not practice what he preaches. Toward the end of the play, Madame Pernelle returns to Orgon's house. When Orgon tries to tell her that Tartuffe has betrayed him and tried to seduce his wife, Madame Pernelle refuses to believe him and insists that Tartuffe is a good man. However, when she sees that Tartuffe has taken Orgon's property and tried to have him arrested, Madame Pernelle finally admits that Tartuffe is not what he appeared to be.

Tartuffe

Tartuffe, the title character of the play, is a seasoned criminal, referred to by the other characters as a hypocrite and an imposter. Tartuffe pretends to be a pious man whose life is devoted to religious worship and moral behavior. Tartuffe met Orgon at a church, where he made such a show of religious devotion that Orgon decided to take him into his home as a religious guide. Tartuffe exerts a strong power over Orgon, who worships him as if he were a saint and shuns his own family in favor of this stranger. Orgon decides to make his daughter marry Tartuffe and disinherits his own son in order to make Tartuffe his sole heir. When Damis reports to Orgon that Tartuffe has tried to seduce his wife, Orgon does not believe this and instead blames Damis for speaking out against Tartuffe. However, when Orgon hides under a table and overhears Tartuffe trying once again to seduce her, he finally sees that he has been betrayed. Orgon orders Tartuffe to leave his home immediately, and Tartuffe threatens him with revenge. After Tartuffe leaves, he arranges to have Orgon arrested and his property taken away from him. However, at the last moment, a Gentleman of the King's Guard arrests Tartuffe instead and informs Orgon that his property will be restored to him. The Gentleman of the Guard explains that Tartuffe had committed a long list of crimes under a different name and will be sent to prison.

Valère

Valère is in love with Mariane. In the beginning of the play, Valère is engaged to Mariane with Orgon's permission. Thus, when he finds out that the engagement has been broken and Mariane is to marry Tartuffe, Valère is very upset about the matter. When he confronts Mariane with the news of her engagement to Tartuffe, Mariane pretends that she does not care about Valère, and Valère likewise pretends that he will be happy to marry someone else. Dorine, however, brings Valère and Mariane together and forces them both to admit that they are still in love with one another and still wish to get married. Toward the end of the play, Valère bravely does whatever he can to save Orgon from being arrested. He arrives at Orgon's house with a carriage and money for Orgon to escape arrest. Orgon is soon cleared of the charges against him and so does not need to run off or take Valère's money. Nonetheless, Orgon is so grateful to Valère for this offering of help that he announces he will immediately arrange for Valère's marriage to Mariane and reward Valère's "deep devotion." Valère's genuine loyalty to Orgon is contrasted with Tartuffe's false friendship; likewise, Valère's genuine and honorable love for Mariane is contrasted with Tartuffe's underhanded lust for Elmire.

Religious Hypocrisy versus True Christian Virtue

The central theme of *Tartuffe* is the exploration of religious hypocrisy in contrast to true Christian virtue. Tartuffe is a hypocrite because he creates an outward appearance of extreme piety and religious devotion while secretly leading a life of crime and immoral behavior. Throughout the play, various characters refer to Tartuffe as a hypocrite and can see clearly that he does not practice what he preaches. For example, Tartuffe instructs his servant to tell anyone who asks that he is busy giving out charity to the poor and downtrodden—whereas, in fact, he is busy trying to seduce the wife of his friend. Tartuffe also displays an outward show of religious devotion by assuming a stance of moral authority and telling everyone else in the household how to behave.

In contrast to Tartuffe's hypocritical behavior in regard to religious devotion, Molière offers a view of true Christian virtue in the character of Cléante. Throughout the play, Cléante expresses ideas about true Christian virtue as opposed to religious hypocrisy. Cléante points out to Orgon that there are many people leading truly virtuous lives who do not feel the need to prove to everyone else how devout they are. Furthermore, Cléante points out that "The truly pious people … are not the ones who make the biggest show." Cléante adds that "True piety's not hard to recognize"; he describes those genuinely moral people who, rather than showing off their religious devotion, "practice what they preach," in the sense that they "judge with charity and wish men well" and "mainly seek to lead a virtuous life." Cléante comments that he feels no need to show off his religious devotion for others to see because "Heaven sees my heart." In the final moments of the play, Cléante again demonstrates his deeply felt devotion to Christian morality, particularly the value of forgiveness. When Orgon learns that Tartuffe has been arrested for a long list of crimes, he begins to voice his desire to see Tartuffe suffer for his betrayal. However, Cléante cuts Orgon off in mid-sentence in order to point out that he should not desire revenge against Tartuffe but should hope that Tartuffe will repent for his sins and even that he will be granted a lighter sentence by the King. Cléante thus voices the play's message regarding the difference between living a truly virtuous life and being a religious hypocrite who does not practice what he preaches.

Topics for Further Study

- Molière's theatrical career took place during the reign of King Louis XIV of France. Write a report about the reign of Louis XIV and his influence on French society, culture, and history.

- The playwrights Pierre Corneille and Jean Racine were contemporaries of Molière, as famous for their tragic plays as Molière was for his comic plays. Write a report on either Corneille or Racine, discussing his biography, theatrical career, major works, and the central themes of his plays.

- The baroque movement in the arts was contemporary with the theatrical productions of Molière. Write a report about baroque art. What are the central themes and stylistic elements of baroque art? Who were some of the major artists of baroque? What are some of the most famous and important works of art from the baroque period?

- With a group of students, pick one of the five acts from *Tartuffe* to perform before the rest of the class. Write an essay discussing how this performance helped you to gain greater understanding of the play and insight into the characters.

- Pick one character from Molière's play *Tartuffe*, and write an original short story from the point of view of that character. First, look carefully at the play to get a good sense of this character's personality and significance to the play. In writing your own story, however, be inventive and creative: try to bring out various elements of this character that are not fully explored in the play, and feel free to make up scenes or conversations not included in the play.

Obsession and Excess versus

Reason and Moderation

The value of moderation and reason in all things, as opposed to excess and obsession, is an important theme running throughout *Tartuffe*. Tartuffe himself is a figure representing the dangers of excess; he is depicted as a glutton—a man who eats and drinks immoderately at the expense of another man. Orgon is also a man of excess, although his excess takes the form of obsession. Orgon becomes so obsessed with Tartuffe that he loses all sense of reason and, as a result, nearly destroys his own family. Even after Orgon learns of Tartuffe's true nature as a fake and a hypocrite, his first response is extreme; he determines that he will never trust another man again and will curse all those who claim to be virtuous. Cléante, however, represents the voice of reason in pointing out to Orgon that moderation in all things is better than extremes; he tells Orgon, "You never are content with moderation … you fly back and forth between extremes." Cléante advises Orgon that the lesson to be learned from his experience with Tartuffe is not to curse all men who appear to be good but rather to carefully avoid all extremes of behavior and judgment and to act less impulsively. As with the matter of religious hypocrisy, Cléante voices a central message of the play, that moderation and reason in all things is better than extremes or obsessions of any sort.

Loyalty and Devotion versus

Disloyalty and Betrayal

Loyalty and devotion versus disloyalty and betrayal is another theme in *Tartuffe*. Tartuffe betrays Orgon's trust and friendship in every way. Whereas Orgon offers Tartuffe his friendship, his home, his food, his confidence, his fortune, and his daughter, Tartuffe uses Orgon for the purposes of his own material and social gain. Tartuffe takes advantage of Orgon's generosity and devotion by trying to seduce his wife, seize his property, and have him arrested. Under the influence of Tartuffe, Orgon himself temporarily betrays his own family. Orgon betrays both Mariane and Valère when he breaks off their engagement—to which he had previously consented—in order to make Mariane marry Tartuffe. Valère, by contrast, represents the virtues of loyalty, devotion, and friendship. Valère demonstrates his deep devotion and loyalty to Orgon when he takes a great personal risk in order to save Orgon from being arrested. Valère arrives at Orgon's house with a carriage and advises him to flee immediately in order to evade arrest. Valère also gives Orgon a large sum of cash to facilitate his escape and promises to accompany him on his journey. Valère thus risks being himself arrested for aiding Orgon's flight from the law. In the final lines of the play, Orgon states that he will reward Valère's "deep devotion" by planning his wedding to Mariane. The theme of loyalty is also addressed in *Tartuffe* in terms of Orgon's regard for the King. In the end of the play, Orgon is pardoned by the King for concealing the strongbox of documents, because he had fought courageously on the side of the King during the civil wars in France (known as the Fronde). Thus, while Tartuffe in the end is punished for his betrayal of Orgon, Orgon and Valère are rewarded for their acts of loyalty and devotion.

Setting

Tartuffe is set in a wealthy family home in Paris, France, in the mid-seventeenth century, during the reign of King Louis XIV. All of the action in the play takes place in the home of Orgon, thus foregrounding the effect of Tartuffe's presence on the dynamics of the family unit. The setting of the play in times contemporary to Molière and his original theater-going audience is also significant in that mention of the King toward the end of the play is meant to be understood as a reference to King Louis XIV; Molière is careful to describe the King as a fair and venerable ruler whose kind treatment of Orgon is regarded with immense gratitude and respect. The setting of the play in France during this period in history is also a significant element of the story. Molière addresses various societal issues of the day, particularly concerning religious controversy. Discussion among the characters regarding the nature of religious devotion and the challenges posed by "free-thinkers" would have been relevant to Molière's audience at the time. Yet, although Tartuffe is set in a very specific historical, geographic, and cultural location, critics have often noted that the central themes and characters of the play remain relevant to readers and theater-goers throughout the world and across a span of several centuries. Thus, while the setting of the play is very specific, its significance and appeal remains universal.

Comedy

Tartuffe is regarded as a masterpiece of comic drama by France's greatest comic playwright. During the 1660s, when the performance of *Tartuffe* remained a public controversy for five years, many critics of the day considered religion to be an inappropriate topic for the comic stage. In fact, many religious authorities considered comic plays in general to be immoral. In his preface to the first published edition of *Tartuffe*, however, Molière defended comic drama as an important means of correcting immoral behavior. He pointed out that "It is a great blow to vice to expose it to everybody's laughter," because "We do not mind being wicked, but no one wants to be ridiculed." Donald M. Frame, in *Tartuffe, and Other Plays* (1967), has observed of this corrective effect of Molière's comedies:

> Again and again he leads us from the enjoyable but shallow reaction of laughing at a fool to recognizing in that fool others whom we know, and ultimately ourselves, which is surely the truest and deepest comic catharsis.

In the course of his career, Molière transformed the comic stage in France, adding a depth of humanity and philosophical complexity to the existing standards of comic theater. Molière's complex use of comedy as a means of exploring serious psychological and moral issues in *Tartuffe* marks the play as a new development in the history of comic drama.

The Reign of King Louis XIV

Tartuffe was first written and performed during the reign of King Louis XIV of France, which lasted from 1643 until the king's death in 1715. The social, cultural, and political atmosphere that characterized the reign of Louis XIV, known as the Sun King, was so distinct that it lent itself to the name of an era in French history. Louis XIV was the son of King Louis XIII and the Spanish Queen Anne of Austria. He was born in 1638 and officially ascended the throne at less than five years of age. During the early years of his reign, Louis XIV struggled through a series of civil wars known as the Fronde (1648–1653). As an adult, Louis XIV worked hard to consolidate his power and eventually became one of the most powerful monarchs in history. The reign of Louis XIV came to be considered the epitome of absolutist monarchy. He combined an international policy of aggressive warfare with a domestic policy of fostering the development of cultural arts such as architecture, theater, and dance. The "Louis XIV style" designates characteristic elements in the visual and decorative arts that developed during his reign, making Paris the European center of fashion, architecture, and culture.

Seventeenth-Century French Theater and Drama

The reign of Louis XIV fostered the development of the theatrical arts, and Molière's career was largely dependent on the direct patronage of the King himself. During the seventeenth century, there were three main theaters in the city of Paris. The first permanent theater to be built in Paris was the Théâtre de l'Hôtel de Bourgogne, which, after 1610, housed the theater company known as The King's Player's. In 1634, the Théâtre du Marais was created on the sight of a tennis court, which was converted for its purposes and quickly became the leading theater in Paris. The Marais Theater burned down in 1644 but was rebuilt with updated stage machinery. After 1660, Molière's troupe was housed in the Palais-Royal Theater. The Italian commedia dell'arte (also called the Comédie-Italienne), a troupe with which Molière's company shared space in two different theaters, was an equally important presence in the world of French theater.

The year of Molière's death in 1673, the king ordered the close of the Marais, combining its theatrical troupe with that of the late Molière and later with the troupe that had been associated with the Hôtel de Bourgogne. In 1680, this combined theatrical company was named the Comédie-Française, the first nationalized theatrical company in modern Europe.

Pierre Corneille and Jean Racine were two

major French playwrights contemporary to Molière. Pierre Corneille (1606–1684) is considered the inventor of French classical tragic theater and was a major influence on Molière. Corneille's major works, known as the classical tetralogy, include *Le Cid* (1637), *Horace* (1640), *Cinna* (1641), and *Polyeucte* (1643). These plays are set in ancient Rome and concern themes of love and betrayal. Racine (1639–1699) further developed French classical tragedy to its greatest heights. Racine became a master of the tragic play equal in status to Molière as master of the comic play. Racine's major works include the plays *Andromaque* (1667), *Britannicus* (1669), *Bérénice* (1670), and *Bajazet* (1672). His masterpiece, *Phédre* (1677), concerns a woman who falls hopelessly in love with her stepson.

Critical Overview

In his lifetime, Molière enjoyed immense popularity among audiences, as well as the ongoing favor and patronage of King Louis XIV, while suffering the censorship and banning from the stage of some of his greatest works, as well as harsh condemnation from church and civic leaders. Molière also enjoyed a popular international reputation during his lifetime, and his plays were performed in England, Germany, and Holland. Margaret Webster, in an Introduction to *Molière* (1950), has described Molière's lasting significance as a literary figure, noting, "in his own language he is as towering a figure as Shakespeare is in ours."

Compare & Contrast

- **Seventeenth Century:** From 1643 to 1715, France is ruled by a monarchy under the reign of King Louis XIV. Early in the reign of Louis XIV, a series of civil wars known as the Fronde erupts in France. After this initial instability, Louis XIV becomes one of the most powerful monarchs in history, and his reign is later considered the epitome of absolutist rule.
  Today: France, in an era of government known as the Fifth

Republic, is a democracy headed by a president who is elected by popular vote.

- **Seventeenth Century:** The reign of King Louis XIV fosters the theatrical arts. Three theaters dominate the Parisian world of drama: the Marais, the Hôtel de Bourgogne, and the Palais-Royal. After the death of Molière in 1673, the king orders the merging of the three main theater troupes, which, in 1680, become the Comédie-Française, the first national theater in Europe.

  Today: The Comédie-Française performs the classic French plays of Molière, Corneille, and Racine, as well as new and contemporary plays.

- **Seventeenth Century:** Until 1682, the Louvre, a building complex in Paris, serves as the seat of French government. During his reign, Louis XIV oversees major additions to and renovations of the Louvre. Meanwhile, the Palace of Versailles is transformed from a royal hunting lodge into the seat of absolutist power in France. The Palace of Versailles, located in the city of Versailles some ten miles outside of Paris, undergoes extensive renovations between 1661 and 1710 and becomes a model of architecture, landscaping, and interior design. Louis XIV moves the seat of French government from the Louvre in Paris to the Palace of Versailles in 1682, where it remains until his death in 1715.

Today: The Palace of Versailles is no longer the seat of French government. Because of its masterful architecture, landscaping, and interior design, the Palace of Versailles has been maintained as a museum and a major tourist attraction. In 1979, UNESCO names the Palace of Versailles a World Heritage Sight. Some 9 million people per year visit the Palace of Versailles. The Louvre, also once a seat of French government, is now a national museum and art gallery of France, as well as one of the most extensive and celebrated art museums in the world.

- **Seventeenth Century:** French international affairs are characterized by a series of wars with neighboring nations of Europe, especially Spain and England. These conflicts include the Franco-Spanish War (1635–1660) and the War of the Great Alliance (1688–1697).

Today: France is a member of the European Union, an organization of European nations, including Spain and England, that share mutual political, social, and economic interests. In January 2002, the Euro, a unit of currency common to most member nations of the European Union, is introduced.

The initial performance of *Tartuffe* in 1664 generated a five-year-long national controversy involving the King of France, the municipal government of Paris, the Catholic religious authorities, and popular audiences, as well as Molière's well-known theatrical troupe. For the modern reader to appreciate the impact of this play upon its original audiences, *Tartuffe*'s circuitous path from bitter controversy to immense popular success is worth exploring in some detail.

Tartuffe was first performed as a three-act play before King Louis XIV during a large celebration at the Palace of Versailles. Although the king himself was pleased with the play and did not find it offensive, he was pressured by powerful religious groups to ban it from further public production. The play was newly denounced a few months later by the president of the Parisian Parliament and not long afterward by the Archbishop of Paris. Gertrud Mander, in *Molière* (1973), commented of these denouncements that:

In other words, the highest secular and temporal powers considered *Tartuffe* to be a very dangerous matter, a revolutionary document which could arouse in the Parisian theater-goers revolutionary thoughts against both the state and religion, thereby endangering the established order.

Subsequent attempts on the part of Molière to stage *Tartuffe* resulted in renewed banning of the play by both governmental and religious authorities. In 1667, the Palais-Royal Theater staged a revised five-act version of *Tartuffe* under the title *The Imposter*. However, with the King away on military operations, the president of police and the archbishop banned the play, closed down the theater, and threatened anyone who went to see it with excommunication. Molière fearlessly defended his play in writing by publishing a public letter in defense of *Tartuffe* as well as sending letters to the king on three separate occasions, pleading to be granted the right to stage the play. But it was not until 1669 that the ban on *Tartuffe* was lifted, at which point the play enjoyed immense popular success, both among theater-going audiences and, in printed form, with the reading public. *Tartuffe* became the greatest popular and financial success of Molière's career.

Over three centuries of international recognition have generated an overwhelming mass of critical response to the work of Molière. After his death, early discussion of Molière's work was frequently concerned with the autobiographical elements of his plays, noting parallels between his own life and career and his central characters. Later discussion was primarily concerned with the question of the extent to which Molière wished to convey a moral message through his plays, as well as the precise nature of this message.

A significant shift in Molière criticism took place in the mid-twentieth century to a focus on Molière as dramatist, rather than on Molière as moralist. Other critics in the latter half of the twentieth century delved into the social and political context of seventeenth-century France in order to illuminate Molière's plays. Hallam Walker, in *Molière* (1990), described Molière criticism since the early 1980s as an amalgam of approaches taking into account significant threads of thought developed throughout the twentieth century so that now "Work is done on Molière in the comic tradition, in the climate of his times, as a commentator on the human condition, and as a creator of theater."

More than three centuries after its initial performance, *Tartuffe* is a world-renowned masterpiece by France's greatest comic playwright and remains one of his most commonly produced plays on the public stage. Walker, in *Molière* (1971), described the lasting appeal of *Tartuffe* as a play that addresses persistent universal themes:

> The subject [of *Tartuffe*] was controversial in 1664, and it is no

less interesting and stimulating at present, because we cannot see or read the work without sensing the truth of its presentation of the effects of belief, love, lust, and power on the human creature.

What Do I Read Next?

- Pierre Corneille, a contemporary of Molière, was a master of French tragic drama and a major influence on Molière. His play *Le Cid* (1637) takes place during the time of the Roman Empire and concerns a conspiracy against the Roman Emperor Augustus.

- *The School for Women* or *The School for Wives* (1662) by Molière, was a popular success in its initial production but created controversy that lasted for over a year. The story concerns a man who, afraid of the power of mature women, opts to marry an inexperienced young woman only to find himself at her mercy.

- *The Misanthrope* (1666) is one of Molière's most celebrated plays. It is set amidst the fashionable Parisian high society of seventeenth-century France and concerns a young man who is disgusted with the hypocrisy, injustice, and overall corruption of human society. His disdain for society is complicated by the fact that he is in love with a young woman who represents all of the social behaviors he deplores.

- Molière himself starred in the initial production of his play *The Hypochondriac* or *The Imaginary Invalid* (1673) as a hypochondriac who is afraid of doctors. Molière had written the part to suit the cough he suffered due to tuberculosis, but he collapsed on stage during the fourth performance and died several hours later.

- *Phèdre* (1677) is the masterpiece of the great seventeenth-century tragic playwright Jean Racine. It concerns a woman who is hopelessly in love with her stepson.

- Molière was highly influenced by the French writer Michel de Montaigne (1533–1592), who is credited with the invention of the essay as a new literary genre. *The Essays of Michel de Montaigne* (1991) is a comprehensive collection of Montaigne's major works.

Sources

Frame, Donald M., "Introduction," in *Tartuffe, and Other Plays by Molière,* translated by Donald M. Frame, Signet Classic, 1967, pp. vii–viii.

Mander, Gertrud, *Molière,* Frederick Unger, 1973, p. 87.

Molière, "Preface to Tartuffe," in *Drama: The Major Genres, an Introductory Critical Anthology,* edited by Robert Hogan and Sven Eric Molin, Dodd, Mead, 1962, pp. 303–07.

——, "Tartuffe; or The Imposter," in *Tartuffe, and Other Plays by Molière,* translated and with an introduction by Donald M. Frame, Signet Classic, 1967, pp. 235–312.

Walker, Hallam, *Molière,* updated ed., Twayne's World Author Series, No. 176, Twayne's World Author Series, No. 176, Twayne, 1971, p. 84.

——, *Molière,* updated ed., Twayne's World Author Series, No. 176, Twayne, 1990, p. 153.

Webster, Margaret, "Introduction," in *Molière,* Coward-McCann, 1950, p. v.

Further Reading

Auchincloss, Louis, *La Gloire: The Roman Empire of Corneille and Racine,* University of South Caroline Press, 1996.

>Auchincloss discusses the historical setting of ancient Rome in the tragic plays of Pierre Corneille and Jean Racine.

Bernier, Olivier, *Louis XIV: A Royal Life,* Doubleday, 1987.

>Bernier provides a biography of King Louis XIV of France, who reigned from 1643 until 1715 and was a strong supporter of Molière's theatrical career.

Jones, Colin, *The Cambridge Illustrated History of France,* Cambridge University Press, 1994.

>Colin provides a history of France with an emphasis on artwork, engravings, and photographs.

Lalande, Roxanne Decker, *Intruders in the Play World: The Dynamics of Gender in Molière's Comedies,* Fairleigh Dickinson University Press, 1996.

>Lalande offers feminist readings of the representation of women and gender in Molière's major theatrical

comedies.

Maskell, David, *Racine: A Theatrical Reading,* Oxford University Press, 1991.

> Maskell offers discussion of the works of Jean Racine, the greatest tragic playwright of seventeenth-century France.

Walker, Hallam, *Molière* Twayne, 1990.

> Walker offers discussion of the development of Molière's dramatic career, focusing on his major works.

Walton, Guy, *Louis XIV's Versailles,* University of Chicago Press, 1986.

> Walton provides discussion of the significance of the Palace of Versailles to the reign of King Louis XIV of France.